Fake News!

A TRAGIC END OF TRUTH!

WITH THE HELP OF MAINSTREAM MEDIA

News@fakenews.com

We now live in a world where everything is fast becoming Fake. From the usual fake boobs to fake designer clothes; fake social media lives with tens of thousands of fake friends, to fake love. Nothing it seems can escape our fake treatment of everything. And since everything in our lives being rendered fake, it is no wonder that our world is now awash with Fake News stemming from every source imaginable. Truth has always been elusive, but it is now much harder to find than ever before. Truth has finally left the building quite literally.

Fake News! The modern-day gobbledygook made famous by none other than the current president of the United States of America during the 2016

US presidential elections campaign, where he vociferously fought against what he saw as a liberal bias media against him and what he represented and stands for. The big news networks in the US did all they could to discredit or damage him without success. Against their collective slander and sometimes-vociferous smear, he eventually won this most hotly contested presidential race against their preferred candidate Hillary Clinton to become the 45thpresident of the United States of America.

Of course, he was not the first person to coin the phrase "Fake News," but he popularised it through his daily rhetoric, which was often aimed at the hostile media during this most fraught presidential election campaign in decades. Today this phrase has become irritatingly familiar being banded around by nearly everyone daily. And so widespread is its use that one is now left wondering if Fake News is something that only surfaced recently. However, Fake News has been around for a very long time; we just never refer to this as Fake news.

Now, Fake News is generally understood as false news, pseudo-news or fabricated news or any news with no bases in facts, a complete fabrication of news. This is the accepted conventional description, and by many accounts, this is what most people still think of when confronted with Fake News today. There are many reasons why Fake News has become so pervasive in our world today. Some people propagate Fake News for financial gains; what I call "fake news greed," aware that any interesting story however fabricated or false will generate more clicks (click-bait), shares online and likely to go viral. Today, any viral story is likely to get more targeted online adverts irrespective of whether it is right or fake. This is what these kind of fake news authors are expecting or hoping to get.

More adverts translate to more cash for writers of these false stories, encouraging them down this fake news alleyway in search of more financial gains. This is often referred to as misinformation for monetary gains, generating a fake story in the hope of making money from it. On the other extreme, some publish fake stories to damage others or institutions. This is dis-information where the false and misleading story is generated with the sole ambition to damage or discredit something or someone. All of these are more prevalent today than in the past, especially on social media platforms.

Many social media users are inadvertently involved in the dissemination and proliferation of Fake News online without even realising it, due in part to our insatiable desire for fascinating stories, especially when they appear on social media. Today spreading Fake News is effortless, and anyone who has access to the web can easily do this from anywhere in the world. The complete dominance and pervasive use of social media further make this a doddle even for beginners. The far-reaching power and influence of social media also mean that any story that is of interest to us will, likely go viral the moment it hits the social media landscape; however, false or fake it may be. It is no coincident, therefore, that there is now a clear link or connection between Fake News and social media, something that social media bosses and their executives would prefer us not to know or talk about. Fake News and social media have become bad bedfellows, and no amount of regulations, policing will ever, get rid of this problem altogether. We the users are the common thread in all of this madness because it is us who generate Fake news in the first instance and then help to spread it throughout the world. We like and comment on all manner of stories and headlines without giving much thought or attention to the accuracy and authenticity of these stories, helping to spread rumour, innuendoes and actual false or Fake News around the world at a click of the button. Fake news creators are aware of this weakness and so designed or write their fake stories with attention-grabbing headlines and images, something that most of us find irresistible to click. The war against Fake News is, already lost despite the so-called good intentions from governments, companies, and various lobby groups from around the world. When it comes to Fake News, the genie is well and truly out of the bottle.

Now Fake News has been around since time began and it is interesting to note just how many people from different parts of the world, and in different levels of society or civilizations have turned to Fake News in pursuit of their selfish ambition and agenda. Kings, princes, politicians, rulers, celebrities, those in authority, and everyone in between have all found themselves in need of a little help from Fake News. People have used fake news for all kinds of motives, and will continue to do so well into the future. Fake News is here to stay though authorities around the world together with social media giants are starting to clamp down on it, worried about the threat this posed to their business models and power. The threat posed by Fake news to individuals, institutions, companies, government or society, in general, is real. Fake news has the ability to damage companies' reputations, and that of individuals or society. Some now firmly believe that Fake News has a potential to create tension between countries or even start wars, alarm the public without cause, destroy democracies around the world, even to influence elections and therefore must be rooted out. "We must be robust when dealing with Fake news, especially online" they declare! Rooting out fake news is indeed a noble cause, but I'm afraid it will take more than just strong words to achieve this and to restore some sense of normality. Fake news is sadly not limited to just social media or the Internet, most of the world mainstream media are today some of the worse offenders of this. This may surprise some, but I challenge anyone to look or listen carefully to news broadcast henceforth.

Our news agenda and reporting has significantly changed in the last one hundred years. There was a time in the past when reporting news was straightforward and the agenda even more so, and nothing more. Journalists were simply journalists reporting the news as they happen without embellishing their own bias or prejudice agenda. In the past, people could be forgiven for trusting journalist's reporting of news events, but today this can no longer be taken for granted. The days of straightforward and of course, factual journalism are well and truly behind us.

Those innocent days of honest, objective journalism have now being replaced by partiality, subjectivity, and downright bias. Anyone trusting any of today's news reports or broadcasting, especially from mainstream media, does so at their ignorance. The mainstream media just like the rest of other media is never to be trusted any longer and anyone doing so is at best naive. Their reporting or broadcasting of news is, peppered with opinions or journalist's points of view on a particular news story. The mainstream media's conscious bias starts long before any editing is meted out. We all know and indeed accept that any news story for broadcasting needs editing so that we get the main aspects or essence of the story without the unnecessary clutter.
However, the way news stories are, edited today; is no longer for the reader or listener's benefit, but in many cases is an open attempt to influence the reader or listener's mind to a particular viewpoint. Journalists want you and I only

to see things their way, their perspective though aware that theirs is often a biased viewpoint. Reading a newspaper, or listening to the news today has to be done with a hefty dose of scepticism; otherwise, you could easily be, misled and directed to what the journalist or their masters would want you to know or direct your attention to and not the real story. Ask yourself this simple question, when was the last time you examine or pay careful attention to any news story that you have read or listened to in the last twelve months, reported by the mainstream media including those from traditionally respected twenty four news channels, analysing how they report their news, which stories get more emphasis, whether they are objective or not and significantly why these stories are, chosen in the first place? Most of us don't pay any attention to any of these; we take them at their word assuming as always that their word or reporting is factual, honest, and truthful. We trust them so much that their word is now law or authoritative. They, in turn, have taken full advantage of our unwillingness to question any news story they broadcast and therefore continue to construe their reporting to suit their ideological end aware that the public will, never suspect anything at all. This is further, bolstered in part due to our over-reliance on the mainstream media for telling the truth, especially when it comes to news reporting.

Furthermore, our collective lack of genuine inquisitiveness or inquiring mind widens this further, leaving us with no hope of ever discovering actual Fake news. In the past, it was perhaps logical for anyone to trust journalists for reporting the truth or facts as they are, as modern bias obsessions did not drive many of them. This was due in part to the fact that the news media was still in its infancy and its power and influence were less appreciated especially that of twenty-four hour's news broadcasts. Early radio broadcasts had mainly government propaganda, something that did help citizens, although not all the time. The idea that any journalist could twist the story or report any part of a story to suit his or her bias agenda was unimaginable. Society couldn't foresee such an eventuality and as such, remains largely ambivalent. However, the arrival of television heralds the beginning of sound bite and of course news-spin. And as news broadcast began to garner more support, especially twenty-four-hour news, the reporting began to change from candid to bias libertarian approach. Most of us never noticed this change at the time because we have always assumed that journalists were trustworthy. We have come to accept the journalism of the past, without much reservation, relying on their honesty for honest reporting. This journalism of the past no longer exists today and sadly is replaced by a biased approach to everything. Again I say the humble days of pure, sincere journalism apart from bias or embellishments are gone and unlikely to return. Most of today's journalists know that there is a level of gullibility or ignorance with their leftist audience, allowing them to broadcast Fake News with no concerned about being exposed.

We have indeed come a long way since the days of five-minute bulleting once or maybe twice a day and that mostly on the radio to today's twenty-four hours dedicated news channels. Today's news is delivered directly to your smart devices and can be accessed twenty-four-seven at any time of your choosing and anywhere in the world. Moreover, our consumption of news has risen exponentially in the last few decades. People, especially young people, want fast news on-demand and with eye-catching headlines and images. Young folks of today do not have patience for long-winded news broadcasts, they just wants eye-catching headlines and images. And the media is fast responding to these demands making fact checking to fast becoming a thing of the past. As soon as any news hits the mainstream news media's desks, it must be reported or releases as quickly as possible to beat rivals. In this new news broadcasting landscape, there is simply no time to waste trying to fact-check and or authenticate any story because the competition is fierce between different media groups to see who gets to grab the audiences first. This inevitably leads to short cuts, errors, and of course Fake News!

The real modern-day Fake News!

For me, "Fake News" isn't as what many have come believe, described or understand. For me, it goes further than mere false news or fabricated news and so forth, much further. I content that most of the news that we now consume daily today is fake, and I am not referring to Fake News on social media or the Internet. This area of news distribution is already well known for Fake News as everyone who is anyone can write any stories they so wish without hindrance or any editorial merit.

All of the mainstream news media are guilty of creating and distribution of some form of Fake news-fact! You see, for far too long now, the mainstream media has had complete handle over the news agenda that you and I consumed daily, deciding how and when to report any story, something that was unheard of in the past. As I have already pointed out, in the past, news media and journalists merely reported the events/news as they unfolded without embellishing their prejudice or bias. They never saw the news as something that can or should be manipulated, massaged, and or inflated for their own ideological or motivational ends. It was the accepted standard or custom, and all journalists abide by it. However, today, this has sadly changed to the extent that it is hard to find any news reports without bias or prejudice sprinkling all over it. Even when reporting on the main headline of the day or so-called breaking news, bias reporting still finds its way. Today's mainstream media are now jostling against each other in a quest to outdo one another, hoping that their rendition of news events will, attract more listeners or viewers. This rather unfortunate contest between different media groups has led to changes in the way news is reported and broadcast. Each media organisation follows its ideological stance or bias when reporting or broadcasting news, either the extreme far left to the extreme far right. However, we all know that the majority of mainstream media are left leaning and opposed to those on the right. It is especially true for all well-known mainstream media of the world. Only a minority of news organisations have right-leaning tendencies, and only some of the time. It means that most of the news we now get or consume has leftist bias locked within though presented as an accurate reflection of news. I contend that this is a **real or true Fake News of today** because instead of getting news without bias, all we get is bias reporting all the time.

Now real/true, genuine Fake News is when a story that is not necessarily false or untruthful, a story that in many respects is true, is reported not because of its importance to the reader or merits to the public or being the main event of the day for that matter but because it fits in with the media prejudice, narrative or bias. Most news organisations have a different ideological position on the news that we all consume though most are leftist. From the extreme right to the extreme left and everything in between, news providers have all areas covered.

Each Media organisation targets a specific section of society, in this vast spectrum of political views, hoping to convert the rest who still holds different views. News stories are often, chosen not because they are significant or necessary for broadcasting, but because they fit in with the media's bias priorities, whether left, right or centre. Many so-called major or breaking news stories are carefully selected and reported based on this bias and never on the level of public interest. Each news media organisation has a slightly different take on the news events, and though many people would agree that this is good for news diversity, this is how we have ended up where we are now, were news reported can no longer be taken at face value. This bias reporting now affects all news broadcasts. Trying to figure out the right perspective on the news bulletin is today often harder to achieve than it used to be in the past. There are no more any reliable sources of accurate news reporting left, and one has to always be suspicious of any news reporting because the same story can be reported in so many different ways depending on who or which media organisation is reporting it. The same story can end up sounding and feeling very different depending on who is reporting it.

Those who get their news from mainly mainstream media, will predominantly get a leftist interpretation of news than those who get their news from say; the very few right-leaning or embracing news organisations. This in turn will form the basis on which we understand the news or see the world and everything in it. Some news media primarily focus or highlight issues predominately on the left while others concentrate on those on the right of the ideological spectrum. Our modern mainstream media organisations are mostly left-leaning and support wholly, or in part, the leftist ideological causes, something that wasn't necessarily so in the past; back then the press were only interested in reporting the news without bias. If a story was true and vital, it was, reported irrespective of which viewpoint or ideological position it may seem to support or seen to support. They didn't recognise the ideological lines that we have today. However, this began to change over time, to what we are witnessing today. There is now a vast chasm of a divide between different ideological positions that the media take.

Of course, it is up to all of us to discern what constitutes real news from fake stories that the mainstream media is propagating to suit their bias end. However, this is not easy given the incredible power and influences of these media giants, especially those that support the left and the almost limitless resources at their disposal. They have a tremendous amount of resources that can be deployed at a moment's notice anywhere in the world to report on any stories that enhance their ideological ends whether these stories are significant or not. People do not have time and sometimes the proficiency to see subtle biases on news reporting.

Today, many of the mainstream media have complete support from Hollywood, and their celebrities. Any celebrity who does not support their leftist agenda would be wise to remain silent at best; otherwise, his or her career would be over if ever found to support any issues on the right. If you keep feeding people a particular narrative about anything even if it is false, they will in time, believe it as fact. 'A lie told a thousand times is better than untold truth.'

Take, for example, the West biased ideological view of Africa. For years and years, Africa has been, portrayed as a continent infested with wars, disease, hunger, and extreme poverty where nothing good ever takes place. The mainstream media in the West started this and continues to pander to this false narrative without shame. Their negative portrayal of Africa has, over time created a view in many people, especially in the West, that Africa is a lost and hopeless continent and this depressing image of Africa continues to this very day. Africa has indeed seen more than its fair share of wars, diseases, and hunger for many decades, but many other exciting stories are happening in this beautiful continent. Africa is changing at an astonishing rate. Africa has made massive progress over the last thirty years, but this has hardly received any coverage if at all in the Western media. People still think of Africa through old negative stereotypes unaware of significant developments that have already taken place and continue to do so. The accurate picture of Africa is unknown to many in the West today because of this long-held prejudice reporting by the media obsessed with creating an Africa of ills. There are people in the West who still think of Africa as a single country rather than a continent. It has been made possible through years of misreporting this continent to their audiences. There are parts of Africa that have known peace and stability for longer than some countries outside of Africa, but because none of this ever made it into mainstream media, the people largely remain ignorant. Go to Africa today and see for yourself what life is like. I grew up in an African village, and the image reported then and now is alien to me. I never experience most of what has been, reported about Africa. We use to live in peace and harmony, living off the land, enjoying the produce of our land; in fact, people used to call our area or region "a land where no child goes to bed hungry." However, such comfortable lives do not merit reporting in the Western media or global news media; the only reporting they are eager to tell the world is always of Africa in need. This "need" reputation of Africa is mostly a misrepresentation, propagated by ignorant media, perpetuated by greedy charities and swallowed by the gullible public. Today Africa is indeed powering ahead, developing at a faster rate than most of the world and soon even our critics would find it hard to ignore. Africa has received a larger share of awful news reporting than any other continent. To report only the bad news stories from Africa and ignoring the rest is to me "Fake news." Any unbalanced reporting of any news story is "Fake news," and the media are guilty of this all the time.

For far too long some may say that the media has had an unfair stranglehold on news agenda and they are right. With the arrival of the Internet, and now social media, their iron grip on the news agenda, is waning fast. The mainstream media is now getting twitchy; terrified that their hold on news agenda is slipping away fast, and are now blaming everyone but themselves for spreading Fake News, trying desperately to discredit or smear everyone else but themselves. They are now openly accusing social media like Facebook and others for allowing the spread of so-called fake news without checks and balances that they claim to abide by. The real reason the mainstream media is now apparently happy to point out fake news on social media is that they have lost control over what material is, shared on it. It is a ploy by them to discredit any information on social media; however, truthful it may be so that users will, stop trusting any material shared on social media. They are desperate to recreate a world in which they and they alone had a monopoly on news broadcast and distribution. Mainstream media has been feeding us the public for years with their version of the news, cherry-picking which stories make the headlines and which to ignore without due considerations for any real news, effectively spewing out Fake News daily. This practice continued for years without any opposition or challenge from anyone. Remember a news story does have to be false to be fake news, only that it is reported or published based on the journalist or editors biased, their narrative and ideological agenda.

Now, if you look at the state of a current news broadcast from this perspective, it is easy for anyone to see the amount of news on various news outlets many of which we have come to trust with our own lives that are fake. Remember Fake real news is when a truthful story gets reported because it fits in with the media's agenda or bias, for example, the reporting or the over-reporting of any feminists stories from anywhere in the world. The amplification of non-essential stories designed to highlight media preferred agenda. There are many other stories that the media can easily focus on, stories that carry more weight than these but are, ignored because they don't advance their cause. Fake news has been the main stable of the mainstream media for many years now. Though the rise of the Internet and social media use is disrupting their monopoly on news, they still hold most of the cards when it comes to news broadcasting. Many of us still trust them completely when it comes to getting news. They've been in complete control of the news agenda for years and still are, deciding when and why stories get reported and for how long. What the public ends up getting depends entirely on the mainstream media of this world. All of their editorial decisions are done by them and crucially for them. They do not want you and me ever to reach a position where we question this. They hold all the cards, having had complete autonomy on the news for years. You and I do not feature in their editorial debate, deciding which stories would make the headlines. They decide the order of reporting different stories based on their subjective judgments and preference alone. Every reporting or broadcast is never about the audience but for the media's aims and objectives. I am always fascinated by how newspapers respond to any pressure to apologise whenever they got their stories completely wrong, especially against individuals.

The story often appears on the front page written in large, unmistakable letters with a sensationalised headline for maximum impact, headlined design to grab the attention of most readers. However, when it becomes painfully clear that this is not true, the supposed apology is buried deep within the pages in the newspaper where one would have to search for it. They never print any apology in the same manner or to a similar degree as the offending story that led to the begrudging apology in the first place. This clearly illustrates just how fake the mainstream media are and the length they are prepared to go to avoid telling the truth. Nothing they do is ever accidental but is always by design. The apology is there for anyone who has time and enthusiasm to seek it out, whereas the offending article was intentionally on the front page, clearly visible for all to see without much effort.

Today's news is, of course, dominated by headlines that only a few decades ago wouldn't even make the cut because they wouldn't have been considered newsworthy or not important. Climate change or environmental issues, all types of grievance, feminists, and now the LGBT stories, dominate our news coverage. These now get the lion's share of coverage to the neglect of the rest. Even when they cover political news, their leftist bias is always on show. The mainstream media is obsessed with leftist ideological driven news agenda. They would report on anything from this side of the political spectrum; however trivial it may be, magnifying it to the level that is will, sound and feel important. Even the way these are covered reflects the mainstream media's obsessions with all the above.

As late as the nineteen sixties, the reporting or coverage of any major public project that could potentially damage the environment, for example, was never absorbed with the damage this might do to the environment, on the contrary, the main focus was on other factors like the costs, time it would take for such a project to be complete, etc. It is how the West was, built; they didn't allow silly environmental arguments to cloud their goal of progressive development. It is not to say that they didn't care about the environment or our planet, on the contrary, they did care very much, but they also recognise that specific projects were essential for their continued advancement and prosperity. Without their ingenuity and careful planning and foresight, imagine what the West would look like today. They cared deeply about the planet, and they did their best with limited knowledge to protect it while advancing their civilisation.

Many infrastructure projects and buildings of the past are today revered by most, including the environmentalists and their leftists' cohorts who are not ashamed to parade them, though they are today vehemently opposed to the development of such in the first place. Many landmarks around the world such as Eifel Tower in Paris, Taj Mahal in India, the famous pyramids in Egypt, the Colosseum in Rome, to name but a few, were built with some inevitable destruction to the environment or ecosystems. Not to mention some of the world's greatest cities like New York, London, Paris, Hong Kong, etc. imagine how much of the environment was destroyed to make way for these great cities. Those who build these cities and monuments were not obsessed with the environment as we are today. Think how many trees were destroyed, how much habitat together with all those living organisms, animals were lost or irreparably damaged in the constructions of the world's largest highways. Cities and highways are necessary for our continued survival and future success, something that even the radical left cannot ignore.

Just imagine what our civilization would have looked like without these developments. We would still be in the dark ages with no hope of progress. I'm not advocating, for the wholesale destruction of the environment or our planet, but for a sensible approach to all these competing issues, the right balance between our needs, that are paramount, and those of our planet. We cannot afford to be overzealous in our quest to protect the environment because doing, so risk putting us into extinction. The survival of all of us depends on how we can sensibly manage our planet instead of the mad rebellion of environmental extremists who are hell-bent on pushing their radical leftist agenda on us with total disregard for anyone else. It is pointless for us to preserve a planet if doing so means our extinction. A world without human beings may be green, but this would be of no benefit to us at all though some people would be happy to see the entire human race disappear, leaving the planet uninhabited. What they fail to see is that the world was created for us, not us for the world.

Today if you want to embark on a similar type project, a disproportionate amount of attention or reporting would be given to the leftist agenda such as the environmental impacts, whether this would impact some people or not. An urgent project can be held to ransom by one individual, and the mainstream media would relish reporting on this,

instead of the benefits of such a project
for the rest of the population. They would,
of course, over-inflate the individual's
concerns even if it makes no sense at all;
effectively sympathizing with him or her
while ignoring the impact this would have
in the broader society. All the benefits of
such a project to society are, sometimes
ignored, and only the impact this may
have on some individuals or the
environment would be emphasized and
repeated. So-called victims are
interviewed over and over again, getting
all the sympathies any victim could ever
wish for, giving the audience the idea that
whatever the rights of the projects are, it
is wrong to impact even one individual or
the environment in any way shape or
form, though we all need it. Supposed
experts are then, interviewed who are
almost always leftist ideologues, given all
the airtime to expound on their
philosophy completely disregarding the
reality of truth. In the past, the
mainstream media would never have

given any time to such individuals because they knew then that progress has to follow. You cannot build a Dubai in the West today; the opposition to this would be too significant to overcome. It is even harder to build a small bypass road, let alone the whole city without encountering a barrage of leftist opposition. There is nothing we humans have done or built in the past that did not impact the environment in some ways, even staunch environmentalists, have to acknowledge this. They are happy to bash any important infrastructure project as a vanity project, but the very same people are quite happy to use it when finished. They do this knowing that the mainstream media would be there to give them total coverage of their supposed protests. This is what I call Fake news hypocrisy.

There is nothing that we can do without impacting the environment because even breathing air impacts the environment.

Today it is increasingly becoming impossible to build anything that might have some environmental impact; however, minuscule it may be especially so in the West. Attention is, always given to everything but the actual benefits of such a project. Those opposed to such are paraded my mainstream media day in and day out even if their numbers are very low or insignificant.

Take for example High Speed 2 in the UK or so-called HS2, only the second high-speed rail in that country, the first being high-speed rail 1 connecting London with the channel tunnel. Many industrialized nations around the world have already built their high-speed rail networks years ago, while the UK still sadly lags. Japan, for example, launched its first high-speed bullet train in 1964 and many countries like Germany and France already have their high-speed rail networks long ago. The reason the UK is still only just started to build phase 2, or the second line of their high-speed rail network is a testament of how much the environmentalists and quite frankly anyone, is allowed unopposed to challenge any major infrastructure project especially those with a perceived impact on the environment even if their challenge is bogus. It is now over ten years since this ambitious project was approved, with only small preparatory work being done or completed.

Thanks to the never-ending consultations, environmental impact assessment studies, and of course the never-ending court challenges by those en-route affected individuals who are allowed to appeal this at different levels of the courts or justice system, etc, it means that the actual work of building this line only just started in 2017 with phase 1 expected to be, completed in 2026, but don't hold your breath just yet, the whole project may even end up scrapped. The mainstream media is already reporting that thousands of trees, which were planted along the route of HS2, as part of the legal requirement to minimize the environmental impact of this line, are dead or in the process of dying. The media is already trying to pour scorn on this project even before any significant works take place. It may be that it is true what the media is reporting about this, but their motive for reporting this is their opposition to this project. The UK government estimate that this project would create about 9000 jobs with thousands of business now with a contract with HS2. There are enormous benefits for this kind of project, both economically and socially. Many people are aware that travelling on trains in the UK is very challenging at the best of time; trains are usually always overcrowded with no seats left, especially at peak times. This project would allow for faster trains that would no doubt free up rail capacity and would make travelling on trains a little easier.

Furthermore, connectivity between the southeast and the north would also increase the economic growth of the north, which has been lagging behind the powerhouse of the UK economy, London and the southeast for years. Those opposed to this project are quite happy to see the UK continuing to languish behind all other industrialized countries and now also some less industrialized countries. African countries like South Africa and Morocco are pushing ahead with getting and expanding their high-speed rail networks while the UK continues to argue about the merits or not of this. The main protagonists of these are quite happy to use high-speed networks abroad without any reservation, continuing to enjoy the comfort and convenience this offers while denying their populations the same, many of whom would never experience this outside of the UK, too poor to afford to travel. The mainstream media are not interested in the ordinary person in the street; they want to continue with the status quo that has helped those running them to live good lives at the expense of everyone. It is what motivates them and drives their ideology. They are prepared to go to any length to report on any story that would enhance their ideological views.

Protests or protesting is fast becoming the main staple of our modern lives. All around the world, many different protests are taking place daily. All kinds of people are using protests to air their grievances form environmentalists to so-called feminist's rights; there is a protest-taking place daily somewhere around the world. However, the only protests you would see and or hear about frequently on news broadcasts are those that mainly support the media's narrative or the leftist agenda. Don't get me wrong here, the mainstream media still cover most of the protests, but their coverage mainly focused on the issues that they support the most or want to promote.

The "me too" movement is a classic example of this malevolent media bias. Instead of just covering all sides of the debate, the mainstream media gives this movement repeated favourable and sympathetic overage, and the reason for this bias is rather apparent. The left hates men in general and loves women and all feminists' related issues. The left together with mainstream media, have developed the idea that women are good, and men are bad and so in any debate about the issues in which women are disproportionally affected or are victims and men are usually the perpetrators, it would never occur to them that sometimes women are at fault though they are victims as well. It is not blaming the victims as alleged by the leftist zealots. One can both be a victim and also be to blame or shoulder some blame at the same time; the two are not mutually exclusive! However, just giving a blanket sympathetic coverage to the "me too" movement risks alienating the very people who can help solve some of the issues these movements are protesting about. Instead of fair and balanced coverage, the mainstream media continue to cover this protest as if men are the only ones who commit sexual offenses.

The me-too protest coverage burst onto our television screens in 2018. For days and weeks, all we saw and heard on the news was their protests continually, and everyone was jumping on this 'me too' bandwagon. 2018 has already been dubbed a "me too" year. Only a few hundred individuals usually attend these marches or protests, perhaps a few thousand at a time, but their coverage suggests otherwise. Just because a few so-called celebrities endorse a particular course of action, or behaviour does not mean that all of us or at least a majority of us are interested or supports it. Celebrities always support the leftist agenda, at least in public, and since most mainstream media are leftist, they receive disproportionally high coverage for their views or actions. If a celebrity comes against or is seen to be against or questioning the "me too" movement or support any issues for example on the right, the mainstream media would ignore him or her, or their report would be criticism or condemnation. Most celebrities are aware of this and so would only support the leftist agenda, at least in public. It makes hiring or getting celebrities to endorse your course, a desirable proposition. The left uses celebrities to advance and promote their agenda-driven protests in their so-called civil liberties war.

Any protest that is seen to be against the leftist ideology is never given proper airtime or coverage and even when reported; it is always a negative coverage or criticism, trying their best to undermine if not attempting to destroy it. Have you ever seen the "march for life" that takes place annually in Washington DC on any major news networks? Most people have not even heard of such a march and all thanks to mainstream media's deafening silence on the matter. It is as if no one attends this march, but on the contrary, this annual march is, attended by thousands of people, and this number continues to grow year on year.   Women and in particular young women have decided to break ranks from radical feminists movement and not keep silent anymore about the mainstream media's pro-abortion agenda. Many young women are now pro-life activists and are proud of this, no longer ashamed of the name-calling from staunch feminists and leftists. For years the mainstream media has thrust on all of us their narrative that all women are pro-abortion, and only men who still want to continue to control and oppress women are promoting the pro-life agenda. We have always known that many women around the world are against abortion but watching and listening to mainstream media's coverage of this one would think otherwise. They wouldn't so much interview a single woman who is against abortion.

The mainstream media does not want the public to know that there are women out there who passionately oppose abortion and are willing to fight openly against it even in public, but are happy to pander to the idea that abortion is only a women's rights issue that all women are fighting for. They deliberately ignore the masses of young women who are no longer willing to accept abortion madness to be sold to them as a women's right and are rebelling against this lousy argument. In 2019 well over three hundred thousand people attended the "right to life" march in Washington DC and many young women especially students attended, but the mainstream media largely remained silent with little or no coverage of this at all. It is as if they are afraid, to tell the truth surrounding abortion and want you and me to continue to live in ignorance belief that women universally accept abortion with no one opposed to it, which is what they are desperate for all of us to believe. They would never examine abortion fairly, looking at the mechanics of it because they know once the public knows about this; it would spell the end of all pro-abortion arguments. Because once people know and see what takes place during an abortion, they would be thoroughly disgusted and angered. No one in their right mind would ever support abortion if they can see the innocent baby being, discarded like rubbish, and the mainstream media are fully aware of this, and so would never risk talk about this or broadcast it. Notice how the media completely covers everything you can think of, especially those issues on the right which some on the left feel are no longer appropriate for modern society in greater depth and critical analysis from every side. The so-called patriarchal hierarchy of society, for example, has been analyzed, dissected and finally misreported as sexist and overtime destroyed by those who hate the natural order of things and all with the help of mainstream media. Whether this system of roles within family and society was right or had some advantages were, never considered, the fact that the left hated this arrangement meant it was, so negatively reported that it had to be done away with. The mainstream media or the press would never find anything good or desirable in all the things the left hates and want to get rid of, however perfect they may be.

The mainstream media has always been remarkably eager to cover any pro-abortion marches though attended by a handful of people, to give the impression that most of us are in favour of abortion. They keep repeating this same narrative hoping that eventually at some point we would believe it. Those who oppose abortion are considered hostile, whose actions need vigorous opposing, but they would never regard those who support it as aggressive though this is evident most of the time. They are quite happy to paint a negative image of anyone who opposes abortion while lording those who support it. They are so biased that they would not discuss any abortion technique in any of their reporting for fear of exposing their murderous actions. If they genuinely believe that abortion is right, why not openly discuss it, looking at all aspects of it. Let's have this discussion in the open to see who is right and who is wrong.

I'm convinced that the majority of people in the West are opposed to abortion, but this would never get any coverage at all as it is against the leftist libertarian pro-abortion agenda. This is a classic case of Fake News, and all mainstream media are all involved in this. When those on the right come out in force to support pro-life marches, the mainstream media either remain silent or would never report favourable to this. Instead, one would find them being overly critical of this throwing all kinds of bogus arguments against this. Also, they would deliberately shift focus from the baby to the so-called plight of the women, who are seeking an abortion, how difficult it was for them to reach this decision, and that no women have an abortion out of choice. All they want is, for all of us to believe that women who have an abortion do so, not out of choice but are forced by circumstances outside their control as if there are circumstances when it is right to take an innocent, precious life. This, of course, is false and a lie as they and all the pro-abortion lobbies know full well, but would be happy to argue this, to intentionally shift attention from the real evil and wickedness of abortion to sympathies for the perpetrators of this, how wicked. They assume that all of us are naive and gullible not to recognize what they are doing here. Every time the press talks about abortion, it is always about the women and never about the actual victim of this. They make a victim out of a perpetrator to further advance their abominable ideology. They callously allow radical pro-abortionists to publicly argue for this bogus victimhood, encouraging even more women to have an abortion without guilt. How any woman can argue that she is a victim of abortion when it is her unforced choice to do so is beyond me. Even their so-called campaigners unashamedly identified themselves as 'pro-choice' cementing the very argument that I am making here, that abortion is a choice that any woman who has had it had to make. The baby is the one who is the real victim of abortion without a choice and not the mother. Even in rape cases, the baby is still an innocent victim, the mother may be a victim as well, but this does not negate the child from being a victim. In rape cases, both mother and the unborn child are victims and deserve protection from society and not murder. The mainstream media would never talk about the unborn baby in any abortion debate coverage because they know that the moment they introduce the baby into the discussion the attention of everyone would shift from the mother to the baby. They deliberately direct all the attention to the mother, reiterating the issues or supposed struggles that she had to face or would face if she carries the baby to term, so that we all have some sympathies with her, not wanting her to have undue burden or suffering in the future. This is Fake News that the press and all mainstream media are guilty of.

Again, notice how the mainstream media cover anything or anyone opposed to the LGBT agenda something they are hell-bent on thrusting down our throats without shame. A recent headline read "Calls for a 'Straight Pride Parade' cause stir."

This headline reveals the mainstream media's subconscious bias narrative straight away, so before you read what they would be reporting, you are led to believe that whatever this pride is, is at the very least controversial. By naming it so-called, they are already expressing a view that this Straight Pride event is inappropriate or there is something not quite right. By the way "Straight Pride Parade" and not so-called "Straight Pride Parade" as they put it, is a parade organised by a group of people who want to see a pride event for heterosexual people, nothing wrong with that you might say. However, try telling that to the leftist bias media. For the mainstream media, anyone who opposes them or seen to oppose them or anything they hold dear is fair game, and they would go to any length to seek him or her out. The people who are planning "Straight Pride Parade" are not even opposed to LGBT pride events according to their on-record public statements, but this does not deter the media who would stop at nothing in their quest to destroy anyone they oppose from writing and publishing a negative story or at least be critical about them. They intentionally direct all their reporting on those who oppose or are critical of this event while ignoring all that support it. Those opposed to this event, are quoted repeatedly to create the impression that no one is in support.

Furthermore, those who have poked fun at this event are rewarded with free publicity to air their views. Their mocking and negative comments directed at this event receive continuous coverage. Reading this article, one gets the sense that the whole world is against this pride event. Repeated quotes from those who oppose this plastered their news coverage, while there was nothing from those who support. They did this to create an impression that many people are opposing this march compared to those who support it. However, how can anyone tell anymore, if this march has broad popular support or not, since the media is always bias against such things? You and I can ever be sure if any criticism directed at anything accurately reflects reality. Likewise, if the news story has many supporting quotes from supposed different people, how are we ever to know for sure if this is how many people feel about it. Whenever they report or cover any story they disagree with; they only quote those who oppose and maybe insert one as an afterthought right at the end of the article from those who may be supporting. However, when it's the turn of something they like, no criticism is ever quoted.

What is it about "Straight Pride Parade" that is so bad that it is necessary to stop it before it takes place. Their adverse reporting on this makes one wonder what is it that they are afraid of; perhaps they think that it would be a success with people falling in love with it, you can make up your mind. If it is inclusiveness and tolerance, they are fighting for, then why stop others having the same fight if they so wish.

Moreover, even after reporting negatively about this group, one would think the mainstream media would leave them alone but not the mainstream media and their agents. They are watching developments here with an eagle's eye and would quicken to report or write about anything that would reflect poorly on this movement. Recently it was discovered that the organisers of this pride event had had glitter bombs sent to them via the post. By the way, glitter bombing is a practice of covering someone with glitter, who is seen and has been known to oppose so-called LGBT rights as a way to protest against them. Their reporting of this incident leaves very little doubt as to their continued bias against this group. They reported this story in a way that one would conclude that the organisers of this straight pride have overreacted in calling the authorities to investigate this. They make it sound like the FBI, fire brigade and the bomb squad overreacted in their response to an innocent prank by the LGBT. Just imagine the outcry this kind of behaviour would have caused around the world if this were, done against the LGBT people. The mainstream media were going to report this daily around the clock, to cement the idea that this group is under attack. However, we are supposed to see this as an innocent, funny prank because the perpetrators are firmly on the left. Authorities were rightly concerned about this because, in the past, people have received anthrax-laced letters or powder in the post.

In 2001, two weeks after the September eleventh attacks, the American public was gripped with genuine fear as anthrax letter bombs were sent to several media offices and two Democratic Senators, leading to the death of 5 people and injuring several others. Then the FBI was involved in what later became the most extensive and complex criminal investigation in history. The FBI, the bomb squad and fire brigade were right to react the way they did, as there was already a president set for this type of attack. So when the media reported this in the way they did, they are by default trying to smear this group further just because they want to organise a "Straight Pride Parade" something that the mainstream media is opposed to. This kind of coverage is meted out to anyone or anything they oppose without shame, further pandering deeper into Fake News.

Many of the world's most popular and influential news media organisations are now fully and completely leftist and are proud of it. The result is the dominance of leftist ideological driven news stories across all mainstream media outlets. The mainstream media is good at labelling any news story as either left or right. However, even when covering powerful and unfortunately divisive stories such as Brexit, their reporting is almost always one-sided with left-leaning sympathies. It is as though they can no longer see anything different through their leftist biased ideological glasses that are blinding them to the very truth they sourced to tell. The mainstream media can make any story they cover to be about either left or right. The mainstream media brands those who are in favour of Brexit, for example, as rightwing nationalists and therefore are seen as legitimate targets by them to pursue to stop them. The description rightwing or nationalist has today become a very sensitive and emotive statement and therefore always carries with it a damaging connotation. Anyone branded rightwing nationalist is automatically seen as racists by the very same media and therefore becomes a legitimate target for use and abuse. This rightwing labelling always gives out the idea of someone who at the very least unwelcomed views and worse poisonous ideas or ideologies. Society has been encouraged by the mainstream media to resists or fights against all rightwing nationalists by any means necessary. So, by labelling Brexiteers as a rightwing nationalist, the media is deliberately creating an impression that those in favour of Brexit are somehow racist or undesirable people, making it legitimate to stop them. The mainstream media keep repeating this rightwing or nationalist phrase daily, to damage those who want Britain to leave the EU with or without a deal. Once this rightwing nationalist label is, given to you or any movement, the game is pretty much over. No one would ever believe that what you are fighting for, and perhaps more crucially your arguments are reasonable and not extreme. There are too many good reasons why British people by a majority voted for Brexit and thereby giving the establishment a right kicking. It wasn't because they were extremist or racist, etc., on the contrary, many who voted for Brexit were mild-mannered ordinary folks like you and me. They were just fed up with the system that seems to cater or benefit the elite, career politicians and in particular those who run Brussels. For me, Brexit was like a last desperate call, an attempt by the people to try and force politicians to listen to their concerns and their anxieties about the state of their lives, their society especially where they live. People saw changes to their lives, towns and cities that has been happening over the last 30 years and accelerated in recent years, which they have no control over, which they never sign up to, being thrust upon them, forced to accept these without qualms, for fear of being called racist, xenophobic and rebelled in the only way left possible. The majority of people felt that they had nowhere else to turn against what they saw as a cartel or collusion between mainstream media and the politicians but to vent their frustrations and anger by voting for Brexit against the very same politicians and media who were telling them otherwise. They ignore warnings from the IMF, OBR, and economists that voting to leave the EU would be catastrophic to the economy and country. There were dire predictions made by those opposed to Brexit about what would happen to the economy if people voted to leave, but none of these managed to stop them. All these scaremongering tactics were repeated daily by mainstream media to influence the vote but to no avail. The people were so determined to vote for Brexit that even the intervention of the then US president Obama couldn't deter them; in fact, his intervention more likely emboldens them more than ever to vote to leave the EU. Those who wanted Britain to remain part of the EU continued to get favourable coverage from mainstream media over and over again while everyone else was ignored or got negative and aggressive questioning especially those who supported the leave campaign. This blatant media bias did not go unnoticed by many who shun their coverage. Every time Brexit debate takes place on radio or television, the prevailing views and opinions were always of those who oppose Brexit. They structure the debate such that there are more people on the panel who support the "remain" camp as opposed to those for Brexit effectively alienating Brexit views and opinions out of discussions while elevating those of remain. Even the line of questioning during these discussions was suggestive and often leading in favour of remain. It was, done round the clock in a desperate attempt to influence the outcome before and after the vote. The mainstream media are still doing this today in the hoping to reverse Brexit completely. Those who preach Armageddon if people voted to leave the EU, though proved wrong in the past are still being allowed to spew out this rhetoric. Imagine if someone had said that voting to leave the EU would make us richer, and it turns out to be false, would the mainstream media still appeal to such a person; I don't think so. Most people in the West are no longer willing to take politicians and the mainstream media at their word and for a good reason. Politicians and mainstream media in the West have let the people down over and over again. The mainstream media's misreporting of news is now so rampant that even when they are telling the truth, some people still consider it Fake news!

It is a well-known fact that the mainstream media was and still is opposed to Brexit however soft it may end up be and as such have promoted the idea that all Brexiteers are rightwing nationalists' fundamentalists who deserved to be, stopped at all costs. The mainstream media have also cynically promoted the idea of many different versions of Brexit knowing full well what the people wanted. They talk about the so-called "soft Brexit," hard Brexit and everything in between to further muddle the truth about leaving Europe. They want to see as much confusion about Brexit as possible. Those who support a clean break with little no meaningful relationship with Europe are then branded Hard Brexiteers, giving the impression that this type of Brexit is callous or detrimental, whereas those who support the closest relationship with Europe are called soft Brexiteers, or the good guys who if we are to leave we should follow them out.

The mainstream media has been trying to throw mud on anyone in favour of Brexit by continuing to label them "Hard Brexiteers." The implication is that soft is better than hard. We must always remember that mainstream media is opposed to the very idea of leaving Europe. Moreover, as the mainstream media is generally ideologically left-leaning as I said before, they purposefully give everyone who is in favour of Brexit or Brexiteers, a thorough grilling while all those opposed to it, Remainers gets sympathetic questioning. It has left many people to ignore the media's reporting on this matter worried that they would only receive a biased view from this most pressing issue in the UK's political history. Now if the mainstream media cannot be, trusted on this fundamental issue of Brexit, what else can we trust them with? The answer is none. It is very unwise for anyone to believe the mainstream media's reporting on anything. The media is merely untrustworthy when it comes to accurate reporting-fact! I am aware that this is a severe charge to make against anyone, let alone news media that are supposed to be truthful. They lost this trust by the way they have acted with impunity over many decades and now lack all integrity and respect.'

There was a time when media, in general, reported the truth without any embellishments or bias. However, today, it is hard to believe that such a time existed. As late as the fifties, news reporting still had some integrity and honesty left, especially in the West. Many exclusively leftist news stories did not even feature at all, people were not interested, and they are still not interested today. Though most people have now reluctantly accepted the many leftist ideologies, the mainstream media still feels the need to plaster their news coverage with leftist undertones daily. Far leftist news stories from far-flung places or countries are, reported though less critical than local but very different stories. The mainstream media would report on the plight of illegal economic migrants with great sympathies and understanding even though what they are doing is clearly breaking the law, going as far as to tread very carefully as not to cause offense while at the same time ignoring news close to home that affects those with conservative views. How they report on the plight of illegal migrants gives the impression that what they are doing is not breaking the law.

Furthermore, it encouraged them along this path to continue to act with impunity. We all know that illegal immigration is rising particularly in the West today, but the mainstream media continues to sympathise with their actions; however wrong they are. Today, there is an easier way if you want to migrate or relocate to any Western country today, arrive there illegally. The leftist media and their sympathisers would come to your aid once you're in the country, reporting and interviewing only those who defend your actions while ignoring those who oppose. Migrating to most Western countries legally today is a waste of time, money and effort, you would be better off getting there illegally where the leftist zealots would do anything to defend you ahead of their populations. The left relishes supporting wrongdoing of any kind, committed by anyone. The mainstream media always there to report this without ever questioning the immorality of their way. Those who try to enter these countries legally and are, refused are sent back without compassion, and the mainstream media would never cover this for fear of telling the truth. The truth is something the left and mainstream media is terrified off and would do anything to avoid it.

Any news story that involves anyone on the right, for example, "Christian's daily plight "very close to home and their now accepted persecutions is no longer considered newsworthy. These are, often dismissed outright and attention is given to other religions at the expense of Christians. Those on the left now hate Christianity and everything this religion stands for. Moreover, one can attack Christians quite literally, and the media would largely remain silent. A Christian can lose their job, their livelihood, business, etc, for holding a biblical truth, and the mainstream media would not regard their plight as essential to draw attention to. Instead, those who claim to be offended by biblical truth are paraded on news media explaining to everyone how much pain and suffering they have to endure due to a single statement made by a Christian. One can use and abuse children of God daily with impunity but say one thing that offends the left, and their hounding of you is seen as legitimate, reported daily to deter others from speaking the truth. Many on the left are aware of this and so exploit it to devastating effect. Christians all around the world are facing persecution, but it s in the West were persecution had accelerated exponentially in the last 20 yrs or so. Individuals from different backgrounds and professions have been caught up in this, from sports stars to business people, B&B owners, to teachers, doctors, etc, all have had that unfortunate accolade of having the unapologetic leftist treatments for holding their Christian beliefs which the left now find offensive. They seem to have the right to go after anyone whom they suspect of offending them though what you said or did is right in the sight of God. They are unfazed by the threat of the judicial system because they know that in the courts' victory for them is always assured.

So much of the news we see, hear or read about is heavily edited to conform to mainstream media ideological leftist narrative. It is the main reason why today's news sounds and feels the way they do because those behind the news have an agenda to fulfil. We must now view all news reporting with suspicion and scepticism because Fake News is what the mainstream media are now good at. Every time they report on any news story, they can't help but slant their reporting to suit their leftist ideological agenda.

Watching and or listening to the mainstream media's news coverage today makes one to feel that the outlook for all of us is bleak indeed. From their narrative of the so-called rise of nationalism to rightwing extremist ideologies and everything in between, it may seem like the future of humanity has never looked so, uncertain. Many on the left are now openly talking about the threat to our very existence from rightwing political ideology or rise in nationalist, populist movement. The mainstream media always characterise nationalism or populist movements in a less than flattering way. It may be true that the rightwing ideology and nationalism/populist is rising but why. Why are all these on the rise today? Is it because suddenly people are becoming less tolerant or caring about others, resentful, inward looking or at worse hateful, especially towards those who look different from them as often reported by mainstream media? No. I don't think that's the reason for all these things. All over the world, people are coming to the realisation that what has been sold to them as liberty, and in particular, democracy was anything but. The mainstream media never truly expose the lie of so-called liberal democracy that was sold on mass mainly in the West and is still being, held as the best model for any country. We thought that we were being, sold freedom, but it turns out that there would be no liberty at all. Instead of the freedom, we were, promised; we have ended up with political correctness that has now infected virtually every aspect of our lives, leaving us with no opinion on any issue at all. Whatever you do or say has to be in line with the liberal left; otherwise if they feel offended they would surely come after you and the mainstream media would be there to help them in their fake offense.

Back in the sixties when much of Western society was in the grip of moral degeneration, the mainstream media acted with total indifference, never calling this out. Instead, they revel in the fact that people, especially young folks, were rebelling against societal norms and custom that has been instrumental in propelling them into superpower status. It is truly appalling for mainstream media to have done what they did in the sixties, looking the other way when society or rather some in society were hell-bent on destroying moral values which have been the bedrock of Western civilizations for decades. These customs and norms were partly responsible for their rise from the ashes of immorality to moral purity that characterise their rise to the very top of civilization. Moral value after moral value was being destroyed, and the mainstream media never shouted loud enough for this to stop, they only paid occasional lip service against this. They were all too willing to go along the many bogus arguments thrown around at the time though they knew none of these could stand any scrutiny. However, because they also wanted this to happen, they acted in total ignorance something they still guilty of today. They would never stand in the way of anyone who wants all kinds of immorality to flourish but would not hesitate to oppose those who seek good in all of us. They are all too eager to amplify any news story they want the people to hear or know about while nullifying the rest.

So when in the sixties there was the rise of leftist movement with their so-called sexual liberties, drug-filled swinging, etc, something the media was very keen to see happen, they never reported this as a threat to any moral values that existed at the time, or the cohesiveness of family and society but covered all these ill-sought social revolutions as progressive leading the audience to accept this as desirable. The mainstream media are never overly critical of anything that lines up with their ideological views; however, appalling. Instead of impartial reporting that we expect of any media or journalists, the mainstream media took a side and covered this ill-judged social change favourably. They deliberately chose the side of those whose behaviour lines up with theirs, thereby promoting immorality. Many in society then were horrified about these new lifestyles that were sweeping through the land with their drug-filled acts, promiscuous, and permissive lives but were helpless against the leftist machinery. Also, since the mainstream media loved all kinds of permissive lifestyles, they just went along reporting this with benign rigor that we now know them for. It was Fake News in its purest form that they are continuously guilty of today. If they had been critical or at least be neutral against those promoting these lifestyles, perhaps we would have been spared the eventual damages this has already inflicted on society. The mainstream media is, at the very least, partly or wholly responsible for the madness of immorality that started in the sixties and continues to this very day. They were at the forefront of immoral behaviour as they are still today and would never give this up; however, damaging this may be to society. Imagine how different our world would be today, had the media stood up against all those immoralities and misbehaviours of the sixties and seventies.

The mainstream media would always remain silent when good and wonderful acts are under threat but would always come to the aid of the immoral and perverse though aware that such lifestyles are wrong and damaging. They would stand to oppose anyone whoever they are, as long as they disagree with you. They would oppose you even if what you are saying, doing, or fighting for is right. They have a strong desire to see through anything they want to happen or are happy to indulge in.

Today it is the turn of President Trump and the media is determined to destroy this man whatever the cost, magnifying and repeating what they consider to be his many crimes even though many cannot yet be, proven in court. They never liked him not because he is an awful person, but because of what he stands for. Now many people may at this point start to wonder if there is anything good President Trump stands for, but there are some good things that he upholds, but unfortunately, almost all of these are against the mainstream media leftist ideology and agenda. It is the main reason why mainstream media hate President Trump so much. Their hatred of him is never because of what they are always banging on, about, racism, sexism, xenophobia, but because he stands for the many things they oppose, anti-abortion, nationalism, strong family, etc. If he was promoting their leftist agenda, the mainstream media were going to love him, overlooking everything that might be, seen as unfavourable on his part. Their hatred of him is so deeply entrenched that they would report anything that they hope would damage the president, however trivial. They are always accusing him of bigotry, racism, xenophobia, sexism, and everything they can think of in the vain hope of destroying his reputation. Every reference to him on the mainstream media is always about accusing him of something, blaming him for something, trying desperately to discredit his administration and would cling onto anything negative that anyone would say about him without fact checking. These would be repeated daily around the clock to ensure that everyone sees or hears about it. I can say that President Trump is a racist homophobe and the media would report that without asking me why I'm saying that. You see, anyone accusing the president of anything would get their accusations aired regardless of the facts, but if I say he is a good man, they would take me to task, put me on the spot. I would have to find unlimited justifications for saying that and even then it won't be enough. What is wrong with the slogan "Make America Great Again"? Is there anything wrong with trying to make one's country great? Who in their right mind would want to destroy their own country or make it less great? All countries want to be great, and none would deliberately choose a lowly position.

The mainstream media would oppose anyone who stands against their leftist ideology but would embrace anyone who agrees with them without any hesitation. It is the reason why the mainstream media loved former president Barrack Obama so much. For them, he could do no wrong as long as he stayed firmly on the left. They didn't even question so much the fact that he received a Nobel peace price before he did anything good in the world. Just image if it was President Trump having received this accolade, I mean the amount of outcry and or adverse reporting would be deafening, repeated day and night. Just listen to their repeated reporting on that old wife's tale of Russian interference in the 2016 US presidential election, day after day they pandered to this without shame hoping that by repeating this somehow it would sway the entire population of the US against the president. Even their appointed investigations couldn't find the smoking gun they were desperate for but was, filled with disappointing and deliberately vague conclusions. Why not just exonerate the president or his campaign team fully. But even with that conclusion they still insist that there is some wrongdoing on the part of the president or his campaign team and so are still hoping for some remnants of smoking gum to bring the president down they loath. I cannot believe that the left truly believes that there was some outside force or conspiracy that was at work during the 2016 presidential race so potent as to influence the final results of the election. Do they think that the American public is so dumb that someone sitting in an office somewhere in Moscow could use his or her social media prowess to make people vote in the way that goes against what they want or believe? The opposition lost that election, not because of some bogus Russian interference, but because people or voters couldn't trust them or their campaign.

Moreover, as is always the case with the liberal left, they would never accept losing, especially to someone like Donald Trump, whom they detest with a passion. They are still in denial about losing that election which was won by an outsider, someone they have tried their best to ridicule and undermine daily with every opportunity they got and of course with the help of mainstream fake media. They discredited him before he became the president and continues along this hateful, spiteful path today. They are trying to paint a picture of a worse president in the history of America with their daily negative rhetoric against him, though his policies are making the US economy to grow faster than most developed economies of the world. Listening to some mainstream reporting of President Trump today, one could conclude that he is the worse president and human being who ever lived.

This negative narrative of reporting applies to anyone they dislike for taking a position opposed to their leftist ideological agenda. But in doing so, the mainstream media deny the public the truth. The mainstream media more than anyone are guilty of influencing elections. It is ok for them to influence elections, something they have been doing for so many decades without resistance but when they suspect someone else of doing so they cry wolf, go after them to discredit and destroy them. But of course, it does not bother them that they are subverting the will of the people when they influence elections, as long as the results go in their favour. It is only when they do not get their way that we start to hear how elections were somehow unfairly influenced, ever looking for an excuse to explained why the people didn't vote as expected. A similar thing happens during the EU referendum elections, the so-called Brexit in the UK, where people voted to leave the EU, something the mainstream media was against and still in denial about and are hoping that this would be annulled and reversed. They interview those who are calling for changing this decision repeatedly in the vain hope that somehow, more people would come to their way of thinking. The mainstream media are fast becoming a brothel of Fake News alienating ever more people.

Most people are fed up with this way of reporting, especially when issues the mainstream media staunchly disagree with are reported. People are fed up with the level with which the truth gets twisted and sometimes wholly overlooked in the pursuit of their ideology is staggering. This callous behaviour has left many wondering if there is any honesty left within mainstream media. Issues such as abortion, homosexuality, climate change, transgenderisms, and so forth are always reported favourably; while very little or no attention is given to those who oppose it. Those in support of such continuously gets favourable coverage and added sympathies while those opposed are labelled bigots, homophobes, and such likes, whom society needs to resist at all cost. You cant even debate facts regarding any of these issues as this would be dismissed at best or completely cut off. The assumption is always that those opposed to these are bigots even though what they are saying may not be interpreted directly as advocating for a total ban on this but merely offering a different viewpoint. I think it is about time that the left and mainstream media, in particular, understand that we cannot all agree or accept everything they support or promote. As some of heir own kind have said some people will never accept such things and so they better get used to it. They can say this and much more offensive statements to everyone but would not tolerate being told the same. This only serves to expose their level of hypocrisy, something they are not ashamed of. If they can argue for what they believe to be right, that's fine, but they need to remember that this is only their own opinion and not a universal fact. Your personal opinion cannot be used to bind others, especially when you refuse to be bound by anyone else's views or opinions. The mainstream media will never be critical of this or all other hypocrisies perpetrated by the own side- the left, but would instead protect and promote their views. Any viewpoint, which opposes or disagrees with the leftist media narrative, is vehemently opposed and the media will never look at it somewhat. Trying to resist the "left" is today a precarious business at best, downright dangerous at worse. Anyone who has tried this would vouch for the truth. Even just passing a fleeting comment about any issues they hold dear can be interpreted by them to mean something you never intended it to be. They would interpret it to support their notion that people are out to persecute or stop them and therefore are entitled to hound and harass you at will. And while they do so, the mainstream media will stand idle by, while you are being hounded out of a job, insulted, and so forth and sometimes sarcastically reports on your plight. A recent leftist headlined reads, " Widdecombe bemoans liberal tyranny" in which the reporter is almost gloating that this poor old lady is having her shows cancelled due to some statement she apparently made. She was forced to defend herself against the might of the mainstream media and their leftist cohorts, who simply do not care about her views now that she has said what they fervently oppose. I don't care what she has said; at the end of the day, it is her opinion or views, and she is entitled to that. Those opposed to her views are free to voice their opinion loud if they so wish but have no right to hound or persecute her or anyone else. It cannot be right, and I repeat, it cannot be right for any society that only the leftist among us are allowed to express their views or opinions with impunity while those of the rest of us are censored or discarded by the wayside. We all have differing views and opinions on just about everything. We all like and dislike different things, and that is what it has always been and always will be, only if we can stop this leftist madness of imposing views on everyone. Some people would never accept sexual immorality of any kind however acceptable it may be for some. I do not think it is right or indeed fair for society or rather the leftist zealots to control what everyone says or do. I will never partake in anything I consider to be wrong or wicked, though a hammer or a gun is held over my head. What they do is for them and not me, and what I do is for me, and I will never force them to do as they do the rest of us.

The mainstream media is at the heart of the leftist zealots who are obsessed with total control of society and will stop at nothing until they have achieved this. Time and time again the left gets away with saying things that no one else can get away with because the media would not so much as question them; after all, why put your side under unnecessary scrutiny when you can look the other way. So, when the left questions long-held beliefs, customs, and traditions, the media not only did not question their motive; they instead broadcast these as to authenticate or give credence to it. So, instead of being impartial and objective, they took the side of the left though what they were saying or arguing for was wrong, and still is. As far as the mainstream media is concerned, the left can do no wrong, and the only evil side is everyone else, especially those on the right. Take, for example, climate change and its coverage. We have known for a long time that our climate is not static but is continuously changing from extreme heat to cold, drought to floods; all these happen all the time and throughout history. Drastic changes in temperature or climate are nothing new or only a modern phenomenon but have been happening with frequency for the last few thousand years or so. It is a fact that you can go and check for yourself. What I have just said the mainstream media would never broadcast because it does not fit in with their preconceived narrative of climate-changing as a result of human activity notably the burning of fossil fuel, something they say, has to be stopped, at all cost. Those who parade this narrative are, given all the airtime to promote this day and night, given privilege access to voice their opinion broadcast worldwide. Even when their protests are damaging to property or livelihoods, or are calling for the extreme measure as was recently demonstrated in the UK by the so-called "extinction rebellion group", the mainstream media would still project them as victims though they are the ones victimising everyone else.

Everyone who has a different view on climate change is shut down, given names like "climate change denials," which the left, by the way, are very good at. The "left" will give anyone who expresses a different view from theirs, a negative name in a desperate attempt to silence and shut them down, vilifying them with the help of the media. Honest and open debate about anything is no longer possible because the "left" will never accept any other point of view but has become the tyranny of our time. The "left" are happy to force the rest of us to take their morality, behaviour, opinions, and everything they love with the help of media but are unwilling to accept any, from anyone else. The mainstream media is now entirely under the feet of extreme far-leftist zealots.

 Matters, which should be regarded, as personal opinions and without scientific facts or unproven, are often reported as factual as long as the leftists are in support, though they may be false. When it suits the mainstream media, they will go along with any opinions or views, including the so-called experts or anyone as long as they agree with them. But if someone who disagrees with their leftist biased narrative raises their opinions or views, he or she is rejected outright or face more aggressive negative questioning that would likely offend the left if ever subjected to them. The left zealots are happy to treat anyone with the treatment they would find offensive. But even when facts support your views or opinions, this would be ignored entirely in favour of their unverified fables. Anyone familiar with any topical political debate programs on radio or television in the West would be fully aware of this. If you happen to disagree with the left's narrative on any issues such as socialism, climate change, gay marriages, feminism, transgenderisms, etc, the treatment you get is at best less than flattering.

The moderator will watch you being heckled and ridiculed for merely raising your opinion, something that you are entitled to, as long as that opinion is opposed to the leftist media narrative.

The left would even dump or criticize one of their own if they veered from the accepted scripted narrative. In their quest for what they desire, they would stop at nothing. There are some feminists, for example, who do not buy into the idea that transgender women should be considered real natural women. This has caused a massive rift between some feminist and trans women who want to be seen as true natural women. Some feminists are not happy that a person who once identified as a man can change their gender identity and become a woman with all the benefits of feminism that they fought for; for many years. There have been cases were some feminists who fought very hard for what they believe in, were being disowned by the radical left for opposing trans women as not true women. Their argument against trans women is that they should not be wholly treated as natural women since they lack many biological attributes than natural women have and may still have the many qualities and characteristics of men. But this is unacceptable to the radical left and their henchwomen. You always have to walk on eggshells when you are dealing with fanatical leftist zealots because you will never know when you will offend them. Now you may be wondering why am I busy talking about this. You might even say what does all this talk has to do with Fake news. This transgender warfare as I like to call it, is a war within the leftist movement, between those calling themselves true progressive and those who only wanted feminism to begin and end with natural women. The radical left will stop at nothing to get what they want even if it means sacrificing some of their own who had supported them all their lives. Now the mainstream media initially found themselves in an uncomfortable position, not knowing first whom to support or favour in their coverage of this burning issue as both antagonists are on the left. Eventually, I think they will go with the radical left as they have always been amongst those who shout the loudest. At the moment, the two sides seem unwilling to compromise, and the mainstream media are not exactly sure which way to go. Instead of just reporting what is taking place, they want to influence the direction of this immoral travel. They are very cautious not to come too hard on either side of this debate, walking a tight rope, so to speak. Specialized programs are currently being commissioned to look at both sides of this debate as they wrestle with trying to find a way through this made up immoral maze. Just imagine how the mainstream media would have reacted if someone on the right had said that transgender women are not entirely women who should receive all the privileges of natural women. They would have been, derided and attacked daily on mainstream media, accused of all kinds of evil, given all manner of names and hounded day and night until they retract this. Sometimes even the apology or retraction of statements like these is not enough to halt the barrage of criticism and condemnations that one would undoubtedly get if lucky. However, since this is an internal leftist fight within a fight, we don't get to hear much about it. Some who rejected trans women have been, disowned by the left and are now left to fend for themselves cementing the expression "there is no honour among thieves."

The radical left assumes that they can speak on behalf of all of us. The mainstream media is unashamedly going along with this belief. Their position on everything seems to be, seen as a default right position by the media and everyone else's has to justify theirs against this. The media should be putting both sides of the arguments under equal scrutiny and without partiality; instead, those of us who oppose the left mindless opinions and views on everything are left to shout to the air with no one to listen to. The assumption as always is that the leftist position is always right and they make no apologies for this.

The news that we now get has changed entirely in the last fifty years. In the past, it used to be assumed rightly that the media or the press would never misrepresent any coverage, especially of the news, but today all that is sadly lost forever. News coverage is no longer what it used to be, just that, but it is now fast becoming like the rest of the news on the Internet or social media. Personal opinions saturate today's news broadcast together with bias reporting, propaganda, falsehood, and quite frankly "Fake News." Some are now calling this period a "post-truth world," a world where truth is no longer absolute but relative. The media has been pivotal in watering down the truth over the years without being exposed. For them, truth or accurate reporting is longer an option, replaced by

a regular biased reporting for their
ideological ends. Fake News is the new
game in town!

www.ingramcontent.com/pod-product-compliance
Lightning Source LLC
Chambersburg PA
CBHW051211250726
48655CB00006B/2357